"'Brave' is too simplistic of a translation of 'brava'—there's so much more attitude and intensity to the term. Brava is just as complex as the title suggests. ***More than just a few stories and some self-reflection, the poetry displays a range of emotions without leaving the reader with deep sorrow because good humor and wit is woven throughout the chapbook.*** 'A veces me pongo brava,' she claims. Pero no a veces, I claim. Garza is always valiant, audacious, atrevida, salvajita, and yes, muy brava."

—**EDDIE VEGA**, AUTHOR OF *SOMOS NOPALES*, 2024-2027 POET LAUREATE OF SAN ANTONIO

"Deeply personal poems that give exquisite voice to the cares, desires, pleasures, and regrets we share as sentient beings. ***Subtle yet accessible, serious yet humorous, Garza's creations are profoundly moving.***"

—**DR. ARTURO MADRID**, T. FRANK AND NORINE R. MURCHISON DISTINGUISHED PROFESSOR, EMERITUS, TRINITY UNIVERSITY

"In *Brava*, Violeta Garza lays bare her desire for 'an everlasting place' to be, become, and embrace. ***Her poems pick apart the textured layers of homeplaces—embodied interiorities, wounded lands, traces, and lineages, as well as friendships and kinships.*** Garza has created a fiercely poetic sense of home that invites meditation on what home holds for us."

—**DR. AIMEE M. VILLARREAL**, ASSISTANT PROFESSOR, DEPARTMENT OF ANTHROPOLOGY, TEXAS STATE UNIVERSITY

"Reading Violeta's words, I found myself smiling because these stories felt like home. My eyes were dancing across the page, racing to get to the next line because I needed MORE. ***This book of poems shows how we are a culmination of our community and of the love we have been gifted by others. They have given a voice to the parts of ourselves that we have silenced, with her breathing life back into our lives through her poetry.***"

—**MARCELA SALOME HERNÁNDEZ**, POET & FRESH INK YOUTH SLAM GRAND CHAMPION (THEY/THEM)

FIRSTMATTERPRESS

Portland, Ore.

BRAVA

BRAVA

violeta garza

FIRSTMATTERPRESS

Portland, Ore.

First Edition

Published in the United States
by First Matter Press
Portland, Oregon

Paperback ISBN-13: 978-1-958600-11-5
Library of Congress Control Number: 2025945018

Editors: ash good & Josie Méndez-Negrete
Contributing Editors: Lauren Paredes, Emily Moon & Hailey Spencer
In Cohort: nawa angel a.h., Annemarie Eayrs & Claudia Saleeby Savage
Contributing Readers: Sonya Wohletz & Andra Vltavín
Spanish Copy Editor: Stephanie Delgado
Copy Editor: Andra Vltavín

Cover: *Brava*
5 inches x 7 inches (woodblock/digital)
Copyright © 2025 by Pearlyn Tan
pearlyn.net

Book design by ash good
ashgood.com

This project was made possible by Regional Arts and Culture,
The City of Portland's Office of Arts & Culture, Oregon Cultural Trust,
and Multnomah County Cultural Coalition.

Pa ma mère, Graciela Garza (1952-2005),
por leerme mis primeras historias,
and for Sean Christian Campos (1979-2016),
for loving me to pieces

POEMS

Papalotzin
tezkatzalantik
tlaj nimokuezouilia
xinechuajlikili

nonan ixayak.

Mariposa
espejo transparente
si me apesadumbro
trae hasta mí

el rostro de mi madre.

Butterfly
transparent mirror
if I feel weighed down
bring me

my mother's face.

—Mardonio Carballo,
  Ni Xochitl Ni Kuikatl / La Canción de las Flores / A Song of Flowers

in the end, we all become houses

after Margaret Atwood

a kitchen
    with a too-short
        countertop,
            a blanket of dimpled thighs,
                a shoe rack
                    in the corner
                        for those feathered ankles
                            that leave and return.

                it seems that my body has transmogrified into
                a quarter of space in a four-plex,
                compartmentalized and cozy,
                crooked wooden floors and
                cupboards sealed shut
                for—   oh,
                        who
                          knows
                            what reason?

                            a window ledge
                        embraces outside's curry
                  and rosemary plants.
              they wait for my fingertips
          to climb and clutch
        and speculate about
     the next forage into fertile soil—
  a birdflight
in reverse.

A Veces Me Pongo Brava / Home

A veces me pongo brava.
I'll be driving my blue Prius,
and I'll reach an intersection
where someone else's car and mine play
a game of *Who's on first?* Most days,
I let them pass. But some days, I step on the gas.
Que se aguanten porque yo no me espero.

A veces me pongo brava.
I'll be at a meeting led by some big shot.
Around me, lots of ass-kissing.
Pero yo no.
I'll rib them
like dorky little siblings.
'Cause I know I can.
Que se rían porque yo no me agüito.

A veces dicen que se me pasa la mano y me pongo brava
y me olvido de la pinche dieta
'cause I want sugar on these hips,
and no one is appreciating
these beauties
the way they deserve.

A list of the things I deserve
could not fit
on a never-ending
scroll.

A veces me pongo—
pos pa qué te miento.

A veces me pongo
tristona,
chillona,
alone-a.
Sometimes, I feel forgotten, like I'm too much
of a good thing for this world,
a shiny currency made of an element
no one has seen before,
much less appreciated.
Una monedita cósmica.

While I was living my gorgeous, incongruous life,
everyone else made
sacrifices
so they could stay with their families and friends.
But I chose worldliness and travel and knowledge.
Y me aventé solita por el mundo.
Y solita me quedé.
Solita que quedé.

Home.
I'm home again for the first time in a long time.
I want to stay.

I liquify my roots and
pour them like tequila
at the foot of a mesquite tree,
the accordion of
Flaco Jiménez
playing through the fluttering leaves.

Híjole. Tequila. Flaco Jiménez.
There I go with the lies again.
I don't drink tequila, and I rarely listen to Flaco.
Just hoped I'd win points with my people.

To tell you the truth,
I lie to myself more than I lie to others.
Can't decide if that means I've evolved or not.
More than lying, I'm trying.
Trying just to be me.

Home.
I'm home again.
For the first time.
In a long time.

In the dark, I feel the wall for the light switch,
only to find nothing there.

Bless This Inconvenient Body

Where I learned
this violence,
I cannot tell you.

Sweet Body of Mine with your pores and paths of poverty–
you are a paragon of patience.
Behind closed doors,
I have suspended
our immense hearts
over vats of acid.
I have stretched our abdomen
so fourth helpings could fit.
Instead of listening to our vibrations,
I have let the Queen of Sensual Famine
dominate.

She beheads any desire   just
                            for
                            being
                            desire.

I confess that I have silenced you, Body,
because you have been
unable to give me everything I want
in the shape I want
in the timeline I want.

Where I learned
this fervor,
I cannot tell you.

I've spent so much time
obsessing over everything you have not been
that I forgot you also have a soul and a memory and a Five-Year Plan.

You have watched me
forgive silent predators
for massive trespasses,

and meanwhile,
I have rejected your appetite
for invigorating erogenous rivers.

I want to say
that I have done my best taking care of you,
but that would be an atrocity of bonestead.

I try to come up with small promises I can keep,
promises to relieve you from the tension of lifetimes.

Your voice, so faint: *Why should I believe you?*

Debilitated, we pause. We listen.

The earth's core slows to a tepid halt.
From there, a whisper—
We've belonged to each other this entire time.
This

                entire

                            time.

We are divine.
We are sublime.
We are muscadine.

We are gurgly.
We are giggly.
We are jiggly.

By degrees, we learn to relish
a new distribution,

sharing every temptation, exasperation, and disappointment,
all in animated whispers—back and forth, under bed covers,
awake and enamored,
balmy and forgiven.

comadre

madre nuestra
que estás en la tierra
mándame una buena comadre
que pueda caminar conmigo en esta vida.

now that i am finally claiming
my chingona crown of nopales and prickly pear,
i ask that you,
madre nuestra,
send me a bestie
who will bring me
community,
a deep sense of self-awareness,
inside jokes,
and completely inappropriate memes from the internet.

in exchange
for you sending her to me, madre nuestra,
i will make space for her,
root for her,
learn from her.

i will respect her
when she shares something with me
that she has kept from others,
in the hopes that she will do the same for me.

madre nuestra
que estás en la tierra
mándame una buena comadre
que me pueda aguantar
cuando me ponga chillona y pesada.

sometimes, i hide
when i'm at my moodiest,
but madre nuestra,
that's when i need her the most.

i don't need an angel.
i don't need a saint.
i need
a comadre.

the chisme around us will be so juicy
'cause we will be so close
that people will start to wonder if we're doing
salacious things behind closed doors,
and it would be super hot if we were,
pero no,
se me hace que seremos
amigas,
simplemente amigas,
y nada más.

madre nuestra
que estás en la tierra
mándame una buena comadre
a la hora que te sea propia.

i'll take almost anyone—
anyone—
but if i had a choice,
i'll take someone

who recycles their paper, plastic, and glass,
who has empathy,
who supports the rights of immigrants, queer and trans folx, plus the disabled,
who believes that science and magic can co-exist,

who lets me know when she needs space from me,
and accepts when i crave solitude,

who, with a warm compassion, laughs at my dumb ass
when i'm overthinking something i told someone else last week,

who offers advice only if I need it and does not punish me if I don't take it,
who is working towards her highest self,

who doesn't have a diet too different from mine
so i can bring her treats
when we're both sneaking sugar
when no one is looking—

but also

someone who likes long phone calls,
and is available for a daily check-in before 10am,
and lives less than ten minutes
from my house.

and lastly, madre nuestra,
no te quiero molestar,
but i ask that if you already sent me someone
with comadre potential and i just missed it,
that you forgive me for being picky
and you send me a bigger hint.

UNO DOS TRES UVALDE

UNO
an invisible hand
rearranges furniture
inside my voice box.

it is the gatekeeper
   that keeps me from
   screaming / stomping / ugly-crying
   my way back
   to infancy.

i don't know that it has my best interest in mind.

DOS
tragedy
   flows and loops herself—
a twisted wire
   that creates a new crib
   of air and anguish
   every day.

TRES
a shape—no longer human—approaches
   wIth aggression.
we believe that,
   in
      a
         split
            second,

we'd put
our love and
our bodies and
our potential
  between ammunition and a child.

may we never find out.

UVALDE
in another universe,
a ten-year-old comes home
from school
with her *most improved* certificate
in hand. she asks for chocolate ice cream,
her favorite, and hears,

si, mi amor.
lo que tu quieras.

Inheritance / Yo Fui Tu Abuela

Yo fui tu abuela
        pero no me dejaron disfrutarlo.

In secret
        but also
        in plain sight
        and with permission,
        I held you, chiquita,
                when you were
        an enchanting child. I kept tabs
        on you your whole life,
        and I longed for more,
        but I'd never get to hear you call me *mi weli*.

That's because my love for your mother,
though immense,
was born of a young, temporary connection—
        the kind that makes
        quesque gente decente
        rage with shame.

When I was forbidden
        from mothering my child,

        I didn't know

I'd also
have to
reject

h e r   c h i l d r e n

in perpetuity.

Cómo me hubiera gustado
ser tu aliento,
        tu alojamiento,
        tu bosque.

Pero fui solamente
tu abuela
y no me dejaron
disfrutarlo.

I know,
        in those later years,
                        that you looked for me.
I know you wanted answers
for the shape of those
translucent welts
on your mother's back—
an unpleasant birthmark that became your inheritance.

I could only give you hints about your lineage—
a coded message
in vague language,
the key
embedded
in our shared
blood.

I hoped you'd understand.

I resent
I could not give you respite
de la tristeza de tu mami. Te lo juro, lo intenté,
y no pude.

Pero quiero
que sepas
que te quise,
chiquita. Te quise
de todo
corazón, de
todo
corazón.

I can only claim you in death,
but I can also respond now with all the power in my spirit,
y yo te voy a cuidar desde acá.

All Things Must Wait in Their Aliveness

for Vicente Garza (1948–2022) and Raymundo Valdez (1948–2023)

My father Vicente, speckled with silence and a near constant susto, crossed on a lavender June morning. His life-long best friend Raymundo—Mundis for short, he of wanderlust and succinctness— followed him the day before yesterday. Unlike my father's passing, Raymundo's was unscheduled.

How curious that, before I heard the news—on a rare, cold March day in Texas—I pulled out my father's maroon pull-over from the bottom of a previously forgotten duffel bag. The warm sleeves nuzzled my skin and wrapped me in a wish for a cuddle.

Last month, I found a handwritten letter from Mundis to my father— yellowing since 1993, all advice and mint on the breath and lines from Kahlil Gibran en español. This piece of paper with crisp folds plugged itself into my family photo album—who knows when—to emerge in February: el mes del amor y la amistad.

This correspondence outlived telenovelas, talk shows, and presidential terms in México—all so *I* could read it. Me, who loses earrings every season, who moves houses every leap year—I am home to this keepsake.

Mundis of the world, of the word, of the war on the isolation that my father chose for himself. Mundis of the strawberry-checkered cheeks to complement my father's George Harrison eyes. Mundis who wrote with such care, even knowing that there would be no written response.

I hope Vicente came looking for you this time.

La Tiendita

pa los que ya no están aquí

I didn't want you to leave,
  but if you had to,
    I am so grateful you gave me the map to La Tiendita.

Without you,
I never would have found it.
But, of course, you led me there.
You always did have an affinity
for adventure and complex flavors.

This everlasting place
    is where I can find a flux of
      the freshest cilantro, queso fresco, and corn tortillas.

The herbs taste cozy, like fortitude, like your voice at its most tender.

I go to La Tiendita
to replenish my pantry
so I can make your favorite dish,
which has now become
my favorite dish.
Savoring it,
spoonful
      by
            spoonful,
feels like having a giddy conversation with you—
just the way I remember you.

At La Tiendita, the lighting is always warm.
The aisles are always wide.
The speakers play songs I heard you sing at least once.

Everything there
is so
vibrant,
even
the wooden floor
feels
alive.

La Tiendita always feels so far away, but once I make up my mind
to make the trek, it's so much closer than I realize.

Sometimes I go there in the aurora when it's quiet.
Sometimes I go there in my dreams.

Every time I go, it feels like I just missed you. Like you were just
there restocking the shelves with all the things you know I like,
but also not only for me. All the other people who loved you, who
miss you, who ingested a bit of your spirit, who will never be
the same since you crossed.

Every time I go,
I think I'm going to weep for you,

and it would be okay if I did,
but I don't
because, even though
I can't see you,
I know you are　　　　　here with me.

I'm always amazed
how La Tiendita
is always open.
However long I stay,
it feels like
mere seconds and entire lifetimes
all at once.

I'm always amazed
how I leave
with the halcyon feeling
that, even now, you entrust
all
　　your love
　　　　　in my palms.

Because you lived, loved, and left,
I learned to be the most authentic version of me—
full of peace, full of music, full of growth, full of medicine.

I did not want you to leave,
        but if you absolutely had to,
        I am so grateful to you,
        for all of you,
        for choosing me,
        for staying with me in the way you can,
wherever that may lead.

/ SEEDS /

// I chose my homeland to bury my seeds / Amorcite Corazón chose
to scatter theirs / in the wind /
                        No
                                one /
                                        can tell us
/ that we were / wrong / to have tasted each other's neck bends / once /

                                        I dig into myself / and find that I
was always a plant with no name / just leaves and stems I borrowed
                                        from others /
Sometimes I wonder / what it would be like /
up   in   the   air
but / my soil is cozy enough / to keep me asleep / through

                                the
                                        night /

I chose to bury / my seeds / in the land and perhaps one day /
        the seeds will grow to feed mountains / salt mines and glass / Today
            I feel so close /
to emerging
from
my
hull / I must / rest and pull myself from nothingness / to a treehouse that's /
                                                        solid /

                                                airy /

built out of paper cuts / and knives /

Maybe / I'll see Amorcite / in

the air / or maybe they will have traveled /   so

far / they won't / foresee /

my fragrance //

Equator

29.42° N,
98.49° W

Juan Gabriel's *Insensible* oscillates
from La Romántica 98.7 FM.

A ten-year-old watches her father
through a dusty mirror.
He runs Brillantina Líquida Tres Flores
through his canas.

She promises herself she will grow
thorns
       and
crowbars
out of her palms.

           0° N,
           0° W

           Under hand-scripted constellations,
           I sexy-walk into the automated sprinklers
           in front of caladiums and distracted strangers.
           My frazzled skirt lifts. Skin jiggles
           in the fierce water pressure.

29.42° N,
98.49° W

She blames The End
  on her vulnerability and @fake.luv's cowardice.

  @fake.luv, relieved upon her exit, throws out her potted mint.

  She, one lonely year later,
  intersperses dirt and hair follicles
  under fingernails
  from clawing her ex's root system to dust.

                    0° N,
                    0° W

                    I mature into a white-braided mapmaker,
                    who paints doors with brush pens of india ink.

                    Never before has this body of mine
                    crossed the equator of her own accord—
                    away from tender-hearted
                    predators.

29.42° N,
98.49° W

After the party, her fingers loosen
her necktie,   remove her large silver hoops,
unfasten her skylight-tinted
button-down.   The rest—on the floor.

She shakes out her graying roots,
studies her nude reflection.

She is all silk now,
all intentional circumference,

                          all moon.

nexus

i. origin:

before
she can heal
herself in her chrysalis
she is made
to procreate
in angular fashion

her inheritance to her child—
  pennies
  photographs
  scars

ii. mother:

she ambles in her garden
wearing a flimsy
white dress

the imprint of her pointer finger
in the moist soil—

in delicate penmanship
those seeds predict
the family fortune

iii. center:

the softest of quilts
a womb of their own

mother and child
explore varying decibels of attachment and warmth—
  aroma of talcum and breastmilk
  on the tongue

iv. pattern:

two decades shrivel

a bird on a branch
 calls for love

a single thread blinks
 unlabeled
 in the shapeless dark

the family once again does not know what to do with it
 let's burn it to see what it is

v. protection:

mother
      and
           child

           suspicious

           make plans in

      separate
rooms

Future Vigil for a Generational Wound

It's dark on the water.
In the shifting candlelight,
      I wear the color of ectoplasm
      to the vigil for what has been vanquished.

My mother's ever-present hair ribbons.
My grandmother's single high-heeled shoe in a reddish hue.
My offering of tobacco and song to the land.

All of it
      disperses from my hands
      across the textured ripples, fans out, waving,
      to pursue a different family to haunt, perhaps.
On to the next congress.

In life, the women in my family line
      had the resilience
      but not the space or the tools
      to chip away
at their tribulations. In death, all their hope rests on me.

They send me
            dreams of coded weaponry.
I awake with words
      that are not my own
      in my throat.

These words
fuse a crystal
of light
to warm our shoulders
across the realms.

Chip, chip, thunk.

After the carnage,
  I breathe out
  without the secrets, the lies, for once.

Embers Inside Strings

for Jeanie Miller Diaz

Just
like all of us.
I keep losing.

Years ago, when us thirtysomethings found ourselves mourning Prince—
   Prince of *Little Red Corvette,*
   Prince of *Nothing Compares 2 U,*
   Prince of *Manic Monday*—
you told me to watch him
   emancipate his electric strings from the fire of his fingertips.
Awwww SO GOOD. I'd already seen the video. *Isn't he amazing?*

The *is*   that was really a *was.*
Wasn't.   *Wasn't* he amazing?

Now, at 6:25 on a Saturday evening, you evaporated from a bus stop
heading home from work and became a *was*—because someone had
to have a drink, someone had to have that last drink. The moon wasn't
even shining yet and lighter fluid spilled on the sidewalk,

        a crimson
         amaranth
            E X P L O S I O N,
      charcoal on tires,
    embers inside strings,

glowing,   glowing,

distant.

Of your husband. Of your school-aged daughters. Of your brush pen
expeditions on inside-out boxes of mac'n'cheeze. The driver couldn't
have known. Your librarian's voice at twice the frequency—offering
storytime psalms to a crescendo of toddlers—encouragement
inside the strings of your acoustic guitar—a liniment for tiny bodies,
fanning their own

purple

sparks.

Could This Be R E S I S T A N C E ?
(Armorial Hanging from San Luis Potosí, México)

A steely celebration of weaponry, made soft by vines and flowers,
with eight birds, each on one foot, reaching for nectar.
This embroidered hanging, engulfed in sepia, is large enough to fold

two of me inside it—but why do I want it to hold me?
There is a reason my mother taught me
to decorate pictures with thread

instead of painting with spears or banners or cannons.
The natural dyes, the jaguar pelts, the misspellings in Spanish:
SEYZO instead of SE HIZO, and SOIDEL for SOY DEL.

The artists? Indigenous dissenters,
who infused the tapestry with pink flora and fauna,
flipping the double-headed bird to the armory of SN LVIS POTOSSI.

aires aires y más desaires

dear future self
i am jealous
so very jealous
of your peace
your love
your cuddles—

from which you
benefit
after all
my hard work

tanto sacrificio

pero no me da pena
ni vergüenza
sentir tantos celos

'cause you honor
the current version of me
every time you
sigh and
make art and
ripple in lakes of embers
and self-forgiveness

This Is the Year I Finally Give a Shit about Bluebonnets

i.

Bluebonnets everywhere, y'all.
Bluebonnets on calendars,
in picture books, strewn all over highways,
center stage in profile pics.
Most of my tejana life, I have been immune to fields
of lupinus texensis—always so connected to mitologías
de cowbois quesque chingones. I would think,
¡Ay, tú! Cálmate already.

But this year—I mean,
damn. I see
underneath. It takes more than
light, water, and breath
to make
life.

ii.

If, on a warm afternoon, I see a single bluebonnet in someone's front
yard, her chin to the clouds, I see a miracle. I see resilience. I see just
a bit of attitude. I see the elders who have long taken care of the land.

With my eyes on Bluebonnet Baby, I draw infinity on my heart with my
finger and tell her, *Tú dale, mija. The medicine is inside you. No te dejes.
This is your home, too. Tú puedes. Breathe for me. I'm breathing for you.
Lean into me. I'm leaning into you...*

iii.

. . . Live   for   me.
I'll be living

for you

soon.

Notes

I wrote these poems in Yanawana (San Antonio, Texas), the occupied land of the Tonkawa, Lipan-Apache, Jumanos, and Coahuiltecan people. I honor and respect the enduring relationship that exists between indigenous people and the land.

Epigraph—Mardonio Carballo's Nahuatl and Spanish lines from *Ni Xochitl Ni Kuikatl / Una Canción De Flores* were translated to English by Adam W. Coon in *A Song of Flowers*.

Page 5—"in the end, we all become houses" was inspired by Margaret Atwood's words, "In the end, we'll all become stories," from "The Entities" in *Moral Disorder and Other Stories*.

Page 17—"UNO DOS TRES UVALDE"—On May 24, 2022 in Uvalde, Texas, an 18-year-old walked into Robb Elementary School with a military-use semi-automatic rifle. He fatally shot 2 teachers and 19 children—many of them Latine between the ages of 9 and 11. The gunman also injured 17 others.

According to a June 27, 2024 article in *The Texas Tribune*, written by Pooja Salhotra, at least 400 officers arrived on the scene. None forced their way into the classroom to confront the shooter until 77 minutes after he started his rampage. This incident has been an inflection point for our nation regarding school violence, gun ownership age, and law enforcement response.

Uvalde ¡Presente! May the babies and teachers rest in power.

Page 13—"comadre"—Here, I honor all the señoras out there by adapting Ana Gabriel's lyrics from her classic 1988 ballad "Simplemente Amigos." I lovingly changed the gender to female, solidifying the song's queerness: "amigas, / simplemente amigas, / y nada más."

Page 28—In "/SEEDS/" I use the term "Amorcite Corazón." This is a direct reference to the song "Amorcito Corazón," made popular by Pedro Infante in the seminal 1948 Mexican film *Nosotros Los Pobres*. Swoon.

Spanish is a very gendered language, with most female nouns ending in -a and male ones in -o. Trans and gender-diverse people in Latin America have been leading the movement to make our language more gender inclusive. Through transnational collaborations within Latine gender diverse communities in the US, this updated language has made its way to us. This is how "Latino" became "Latinx/Latine." Overall, choosing to end nouns in -e is less confusing than -x, because it is easier to pronounce—hence the gender-neutral noun "Amorcite."

Page 30—In "Equator," I make reference to an old-school hair product called "brillantina." It smooths hair and gets flyaways to stop singing so loud, so to speak. I grew up seeing a little bottle of the Tres Flores brand on my parents' dresser, which eventually made my father's canas (white hair/grays) slightly yellow from overuse. I ask to have a full head of canas to show off one day.

Page 41—"Embers Inside Strings" was written for my former co-worker, Jeanie Miller Diaz, a youth librarian for the Multnomah County Library, Portland, Oregon. In 2023, while waiting at the bus stop at the end of her shift, she was struck and killed by a drunk driver at the age of 43. At least once, we openly dreamed about what life would be like if we could just be full-time artists. Jeanie, may you continue to make beautiful things from Spirit Side, sweet friend.

Page 43—The poem "Could This Be R E S I S T A N C E ? (Armorial Hanging from San Luis Potosí, México)" was my response to the 2023 Ekphrastic Poetry Contest, run by National Poetry Month San Antonio. I wrote a poem about a 1771 armorial hanging at the San Antonio Museum of Art, and it was one of the winners. The medium is listed as "cotton and wool embroidery on linen ground, natural dyes," and the dimensions are 93 ⅛ x 90 ½ in (236 x 229.9 cm).

Acknowledgments

I would like to acknowledge and thank the editors of the following journals and anthologies, who published these poems in the original or early stages of their birth:

The ASP Bulletin: "in the end, we all become houses"
Acentos Review: "A Veces Me Pongo Brava / Home"
Journal X: "comadre"
Arts Alive San Antonio: "UNO DOS TRES UVALDE"
Zoetic Press / Heathentide Orphans 2025 anthology: "Inheritance / Yo Fui Tu Abuela"
Samsara Magazine: "La Tiendita"
Moist Poetry Journal: "/SEEDS/"
Not Ghosts, But Spirits (vol. II): "Equator" and "Future Vigil for a Generational Wound"
Monterey Poetry Review: "Future Vigil for a Generational Wound"
riverSedge: A Journal of Art and Literature: "Could This Be RESISTANCE? (Armorial Hanging from San Luis Potosí, México)"
Cuéntame Literary Magazine: "aires aires y más desaires"
Voices de la Luna: "This Is the Year I Finally Give a Shit about Bluebonnets"
Under the Lens: A Sound Performance of Poetry and Art: "This Is the Year I Finally Give a Shit about Bluebonnets"

––––––––

I first want to thank you, esteemed reader, for witnessing this work. May the experience bloom something audacious within you. I want to extend my love to my First Matter Press cohort—

Annemarie Eayrs, Claudia Saleeby Savage, and nawa angel a.h.—plus the dynamite FMP editors who helped finesse my manuscript—Emily Moon, Lauren Paredes, Hailey Spencer, Josie Méndez-Negrete, Andra Vltavín, and Sonya Wohletz. I am especially grateful to the solstice and equinox moondust that brought me to ash good. The universe brought us together in friendship and poetry so we could create this exquisite badassery. I humbly receive.

Mil gracias de todo corazón to my editor and poetry book therapist—el más chingón, John Olivares Espinoza. To this list, I must add my Spanish language editor, Stephanie Delgado, and my Uvalde sensitivity reader, Stephanie Hinojosa. Órale, adelante siempre.

I am in awe of the incredible writing groups who have taken me in during the past few years—Macondo Writers Workshop, Poesía y Jotería Queer Spanglish Poetry Group, Wyrdd Writers, Deepening Our Listening Poetry Circle, Twinklelight Poetry Group, Bereket Writers, Women Who Submit—San Antonio, High Priestesses of Poetry, and Teatro Esperanza. You are all so lovely to me. A very special thank you to Rigoberto González, Lisha Adela García, Cyra Dumitru, and Sevde Kaldiroglu for your leadership in creating invigorating spaces for our poetic little hearts. To this list, I must include Jess Kadish-Hernández, Monique Ngozi Nri, and Brian O'Sullivan, Ph.D., for your always charming support of my work. Also, thank you to Jean Hackett and Annie Snider for providing brief word lists for "All Things Must Wait in Their Aliveness" and "Future Vigil for a Generational Wound."

And where would I be without my literary confidants? In the dark, I called, and you all came with your chisme, dreams, and sweetness. Carmen Calatayud, Desiree Kannel, and Osmani Ochoa, you are prayers come to life.

In 2019, I hit my head on a bookshelf, causing my first traumatic brain injury. To my Constellation of Concussions: as intensely painful as you have been, you amaze me. You gave me the confidence to call myself a poet. You are my greatest teacher.

My deepest gratitude to my Ancestors—some of y'all are still teaching me, with so much love, what it means to be bra-va, jajaja. I also send much love to my living family members, especially Josué and Gabriela. Thank you for being you.

Y finalmente, mi amorrrrrr Barbie Hurtado, te quiero tres chingos. Our Ancestors root for us every time we cuddle in each other's arms. Gracias por enseñarme lo que es el amor verdaderamente bonito.

A multilingual poet, educator and performance doula, **VIOLETA GARZA** is the textbook middle child in a family of Mexican immigrants. Her work has been published in *Anti-Heroin Chic*, *Foglifter*, and *Acentos Review*, among others. They have performed their original poems and stories for Texas Public Radio, The Alamo Chapter for Human Rights, The Center for Refugee Services, and elsewhere. A member of the Macondo Writers Workshop, she lives a sweet, queer life in Yanawana (San Antonio, Texas), with her partner and an adequate number of potted plants. See her work at violetagarza.com

2025
FEATURED ARTIST PEARLYN TAN

WALING WALING PALPITATIONS
nawa angel a.h.

THE DYING ROOM
RECIPIENT OF THE PRIMA MATERIA AWARD
annemarie eayrs

BRAVA
violeta garza

FIRST YOU MUST DESTROY THE WORLD
claudia saleeby savage

2024
FEATURED ARTIST ALEXANDRA STRENFEL

GREENHOUSE
sophie hall

SUSPENDED IN MY INSECTICIDE JAR
clara mcauley

2023
FEATURED ARTIST LARA ROUSE

FLOATING BONES
rae diamond

TEN-CENT FLOWER & OTHER TERRITORIES
charity e. yoro

OUR FAVORITE PEOPLE IN THE ROOM
edited by ash good, lauren paredes & emily moon

2022
FEATURED ARTIST RACHEL MULDER

BETWEEN THESE BORDERS WANDERS A GOLEM
ahuva s. zaslavsky

EVEN THE AIR, TOO HEAVY
riley danvers

ONE ROW AFTER / BIR SIRA SONRA
sonya wohletz

SOMEONE I CAN HOLD GENTLY
xylophone mykland

STORIES FOR WHEN THE WOLVES ARRIVE
hailey spencer

2021

CONSIDER THE BODY, WINGED
jessica e. pierce

ROUTES BETWEEN RAINDROPS
dan wiencek

THE GROWTH LINES
gabby hancher

2020

BODY UNTIL LIGHT
k.m. lighthouse

IT'S JUST YOU & ME, MISS MOON
emily moon

LOVERS AND OTHER STILL CREATURES
eitan codish

2019

OTHERWISE, MAGIC
lauren paredes

THE NIGHT SKY IS A PLACE WHERE THINGS GET LOST
andrew chenevert

TIME COUNTS BACKWARD FROM INFINITY
k.m. lighthouse

WE ARE NOT READY FOR WHAT WE ARE
ash good

2018

SOUNDS IN MY MÖBIUS MIND
ash good

YOU ARE AN AMBIGUOUS PRONOUN
k.m. lighthouse

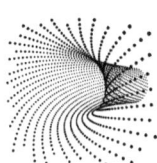

FIRSTMATTERPRESS
Portland, Ore.